ENDORSEMENTS

"What if you didn't get one chance to make a first impression, but many? You do! Steven Littlefield shows us how to use the magic power of personal stories to create life-lasting relationships one impression at a time."
—Mike Michalowicz, author of *Profit First*

"A delightful, must-read guide chock full of critically important information that will help anyone seeking to create and deepen successful business and personal relationships."
—Walt Hampton, JD, best-selling author of *Journeys on the Edge* and *The Power Principles of Time Mastery*, and president of Book Yourself Solid® Worldwide

"If you want to increase your likability, implement Steven Littlefield's thank-you note system outlined in *The Business of Gratitude*. By the end of the year, you will have more than 1,800 deeper relationships."
—Michael Port, *Wall Street Journal* best-selling author of *Steal the Show*

"Gratitude and the handwritten thank-you note? How do you build a book around that? That's what I thought the first time the idea was floated past me. But that was before I heard the story behind it all. Before I learned that something so simple could totally switch up not just your business, but the way you operate in the world. You need to read this book. Simple or not, I guarantee the ideas in here will change your life."

—Ann Sheybani Hampton,
author of *How to Eat the Elephant*

"As a chairman of the board of a Fortune 1000 corporation, I have skimmed a lot of books on sales, marketing, and improving individual performance. But *The Business of Gratitude* grabbed me from the beginning and forced me to read to the very end. It offers a foolproof process that creates predictable results. In this impersonal age of tweets, texts, emails, and automated consumer contact systems, the handwritten note is the new disruptive app."

—Dave Agena, international mortgage
banking executive and former chairman of
the board of MGIC Australia

"*The Business of Gratitude* is an invaluable book! Frankly, this is an area I'm not strong in, and I can just imagine how beneficial using Steven Littlefield's gratitude techniques would have been to me had I applied them throughout my career. Don't make that same mistake. Start applying these critical ideas in your life immediately!"

—Vic Conant, president of NightingaleConant.com and world leader in audio personal achievement

"If you want a system to deepen the relationships with the people around you or you want to attract new people to hang around, read *The Business of Gratitude* and implement the steps Steven Littlefield has outlined for you. I know his system works, because Steven and I have been friends for more than twenty-five years."

—Marshall Sylver, the Millionaire Maker

"Steven Littlefield has written an exceptional book on one of the most powerful tools anyone can apply to business and to life."

—Tom Hopkins, author of *How to Master the Art of Selling*

The
Business
of
Gratitude

Abundance through Gratitude and the Handwritten Thank-You Note

STEVEN A. LITTLEFIELD

Josh,

Who can you thank today?

Absolute Results Publishing

Published by Absolute Results Publishing
Copyright © 2017 by Steven A. Littlefield
All rights reserved.

Absolute Results Publishing
11234 El Camino Real #100
San Diego, CA 92130
E-mail: AbsoluteResultsPub@gmail.com

Limit of Liability/Disclaimer of Warranty:

Publishing and editorial team: Author Bridge Media, www.AuthorBridgeMedia.com
Project Manager and Editorial Director: Helen Chang
Editor: Katherine MacKennett
Publishing Manager: Laurie Aranda
Publishing Assistant: Iris Sasing
Cover design: James Subramanian

We put the international symbol of gratitude in the center using the background color for gratitude and thankfulness of dark pink. We utilized white space for access into the infinite and lower case lettering to show reverence to our universal connectedness.

Library of Congress Control Number: 2016921395
ISBN: 978-0-9985072-0-0 -- paperback
978-0-9985072-1-7 -- hardcover
978-0-9985072-2-4 -- ebook
978-0-9985072-3-1 -- audiobook

Ordering Information:

Quantity sales. Special discounts are available on quantity purchases by corporations, associations, and others. For details, contact the publisher at the address above.

Printed in the United States of America

DEDICATION

To my mom Atherlyn J. Littlefield
For your love, creativity, and inspiration.
To my dad Theodore J. Littlefield
For your love, compassion, and instilling in me
the insatiable desire to read, learn & teach.
To my mother Judy Ferris Dern for your love and
giving birth to me.

ACKNOWLEDGMENTS

Stephen Covey, in his book *The 7 Habits of Highly Effective People*, said, "Begin with the end in mind." This book would not have gone from idea to published without my friend Helen Chang at Author Bridge Media and her amazing team. Thank you to Katherine MacKenett for her amazing editing skills and insight, Laurie Aranda for her organizational skills, Iris Sasing for keeping me accountable and on track, and Vanessa Black, whose passion for taking ideas to published book was infectious. Our designer, James Subramanian, was very patient with the changes I requested and created our beautiful cover.

My thanks also go to Christine Messier, who encouraged me to put pen to paper and began this project with me by taking my longhand writings on a legal pad to begin the process and instilled the belief in me that I could draw this book out of me. Thanks also to my creative writer, Ann Sheybani-Hampton, who helped me find the passion for this book, guiding me through "pain island" and "pleasure island" in order to weave my story into the system of handwritten thank-you notes and why it is important. I am grateful for my mentors, Michael Port and Mike Michalowicz, for creating the book boat retreat, where I learned the behind-the-scenes process of getting a book published and how to market a book so it actually gets in the hands of you, the reader. I am also grateful to my friends and family for their encouragement, input, and infusion of love for *The Business of Gratitude*!

Finally, it is an honor and privilege to credit Tom Hopkins who created the phraseology and wording for the foundation of these handwritten thank you notes.

I also want to thank my sponsors

My Platinum Sponsors:

Bruce A. Hofbauer, David B. Littlefield, DDS, Don, Valerie, Connor and Trevor Gasgarth

Jenjer L. Wind, Livingston Family Trust, Londa L. Gregg, R. M. Hasson, Robert A. Ilse

My Gold Sponsors:

Charles Butler, Yvette and Dan Charlton, DDS, Kath and Dirk Broekema, Jacque and Doug Eisold, Jay Hibert, Meghan Federico, Your Loan Ladies

My Silver Sponsors:

James Green, Ken Grabow, M.D., Marilyn Winters, Kevin Willenborg, Pat and Greg Alston-Aldrich, Steve Vande Vegte, Thomas, Kerry and Chandler Reid

My Bronze Sponsors:

Jack Atkinson, Jesse Adams, Mary and Kelly Jones, Killu Sanbor

CONTENTS

FOREWORD

In the early '80s, we were poised to take over the world. I was the lead singer in the Canadian rock band Loverboy. Our singles blasted from every radio station and shot up the charts on MTV. Maybe you remember "Working for the Weekend" and "Lucky Ones." Unbelievable, our good fortune.

When you're a rock star, people are grabbing at you all the time. Everybody wants to be your buddy, to do deals with you, to pitch you their project. Everybody's working you. There's a lot of white noise, so it's easy to tune out. It took a lot to get my attention.

One day, I received a handwritten thank-you note from Steven, whom I'd met at a celebrity golf tournament. He seemed genuinely appreciative of the opportunity to hang out, to share some laughs on the links. He didn't want anything from me; he was just showing some gratitude and being human. He'd included his contact information, so I texted him back. Why not? We've been pals ever since.

Truth is, until I read this book, I had forgotten exactly how our friendship began. That's how long it's been.

That handwritten thank-you note, though, opened the door. Steven waltzed in right past the security crew. He was one of those rare dudes with follow-through. There are no guarantees that when you reach out to someone anything will come of it. But it sure won't happen if you don't.

Only the lucky ones get to steal the show. Only the lucky ones know.

Don't wait to get lucky; make your own luck. That's how this game is played.

Steven has developed a method to get lucky in business, in life, and in friendships. He can show you how to hit the big time, how to take the prize. He's got a system that combines gratitude and connection with strategy and discipline, with follow-through.

Do what the man tells you to do.

You don't make it in the music industry unless you can show gratitude to an audience, unless you can get personal from the stage. I'm a grateful guy. I'm not grateful just for my audience, but also for the chance to sing my songs (I don't care if I'm in Paris, France, or Perris, California), for my bandmates, for those moments when I come alive.

If you're a businessperson, you're in the gratitude business too. Only you work from the small stage, one on one. You need to go out of your way to get personal with people. You want your audience to open up. You've got to get personal with every show. You've got to thank them every chance you get. Watch how it changes your life.

You want a piece of my heart?
You better start from the start
You want to be in the show?
C'mon baby, let's go

—Mike Reno

INTRODUCTION

The Day It All Went Wrong

Just after seven o'clock in the morning, a knock sounded on the second-floor door of my fraternity room.

It was May 3, 1984. I opened the door and a man in his forties with a bad sports jacket asked, "Are you Steven Littlefield?"

"I am." I had just finished brushing my teeth so I could walk to my last final exam of college, which was scheduled for 8:00 a.m. Calculus II was the only credit I needed to receive my bachelor of science degree in chemistry with an emphasis in biochemistry. All the seniors had to take their exams a week early so they could be graded in time for us to receive our diplomas at graduation.

"Do you own a white Mercedes Benz 230SL convertible?" he asked.

I told him I did. He asked me to accompany him as there had been an incident with my car in the parking lot. I stepped out of my room to follow him down the back stairs leading to the parking lot. When I did, another man stepped in behind me. As we exited the building, the man with the bad sports jacket spoke up again.

"Your car is fine," he said. "But we need to talk to you."

They escorted me to the back seat of their vehicle and sat on either side of me. The first introduced himself as officer So-and-So and started talking to me in a fatherly manner. A search warrant had been served, and other officers were currently turning my room upside down, he explained. He knew that I was adopted and that I wanted to make my parents proud. That I wanted to go to medical school. That I wasn't a bad kid—I had just got caught up with the "wrong crowd."

Someone knocked on the window. The officer excused himself and stepped outside.

When he got back in, he told me I was under arrest for the possession of cocaine and read me my rights.

Everything seemed to slow down. I thought I was going to throw up. I thought about Roy, my best friend and fraternity brother. Roy had been the one who'd taken it upon himself to prove to the brotherhood that I was fraternity material. He'd popped open the first beer I'd ever drunk. I was introduced to cocaine at the frat house. As a Seventh-day Adventist who'd never done anything like this before, the feeling that I could drink, snort cocaine, and not pass out was exciting. It created some lively discussions.

One night around 2:00 a.m. when we were drinking, Roy and I jumped in his car and cruised to the risky side of town to get some cocaine. "Why don't we have cocaine on hand so that we don't have to drive around drunk in the middle of the night, putting ourselves at risk?" I asked him. I started pre-buying it so that we'd never have to do that again. Then the secret got out. Before long, I had a handful of select customers.

That's how a good boy like me had become a drug dealer.

Now, my mistake had caught up with me. *How had I ended up in this situation?* I was about to graduate from college. Instead of getting my degree and going on to med school, my sentence was one year in prison. Even after I got out of jail, I would have a felony on my record—permanently.

Life as I knew it was over.

Stuck

In our culture, we've been taught that success depends heavily on graduating from college with a respectable GPA, pursuing a graduate degree (preferably in law or medicine), and then working twenty-hour days for the next forty years without complaint—all the while forgoing meaningful relationships and fun in the name of material wealth.

What if you can't take this guaranteed path to "success" because you've screwed up like me?

Or what if, given the choice, you reject this path because you want your life to matter? Because you don't want to just sit in one of those cubicle fields and fade into the scene?

Because you want success, but not at the expense of purpose and connection? What if, more than anything, you want to have relationships that truly matter, to work with people you actually like, and to have fun?

You want the big house, the exotic vacations, and the sports cars, but you don't want to kiss butt or crush fingers on your lonely climb up the ladder. Or if you've taken the traditional route and have been doing all the "right" things, you find yourself worried that you're going to end up mired in some soulless career in the end.

You want success, but you can't stomach the thought of losing your freedom, your integrity, or your soul.

You wish you could completely switch course. Pursue what you love. Build a business serving people you enjoy. But how?

How do you achieve real success without selling yourself down the river?

There is another way, and by necessity, I found it. I'm going to pull back the curtain and show you my secret path. It's always been there, but over time, it's been forgotten.

Until now.

Gratitude Makes a Way

Here's the real question: If you could do one thing that took under five minutes and made an enormous personal impression on someone, would you do it? If this one thing was the lynchpin to the kind of success you're after, would you take on the task and work it like it's your job?

Now, what if I told you that the lynchpin is simply the handwritten thank-you note?

It is. And it works.

On the surface it seems simple, but consider this for a moment. If you can differentiate yourself enough to turn the people you meet into friends and clients, you can create success. Success on your terms, which means doing business the way you want, with whom you want.

That's the outcome we're after.

I have found that the simple handwritten thank-you note is the cornerstone of my business. It is the key to my success—despite being a man with two strikes against him. This tool has allowed me to create valuable relationships, inspire loyalty, demonstrate integrity, prove that gratitude leads to abundance, set myself apart from the herd, keep me front and center in the minds of decision makers, and add to my reputation of professionalism, consistency, dependability, and attention to detail.

This is how you win this success game.

With the handwritten thank-you note system, you never have to settle for success that's not on your terms again. All of the opportunities that lie beyond the small effort of sending a note become yours to capture and enjoy. And some of these opportunities are more incredible than you can imagine.

Sending thank-you cards seems super simple. The first

time I heard about it, I thought it was too simple. It didn't involve hours out of my day or learning some complicated technology, and it didn't cost a lot of money. Shouldn't success come at a much higher expense?

Apparently not. And I've been fortunate enough to experience it firsthand.

The Business of Thank You

For the last thirty years, I have lived and breathed thank-you notes.

I'm in the mortgage loan business. The simple thank-you card is the cornerstone of Signature Funding, the multimillion-dollar business I built with my partner, Jenjer, that has funded more than $3 billion in home loans. By 2006, we were 165 employees funding hundreds of loans a month with loan closings of more than $800 million a year. In 2006, a substantial investment banking company offered us $10 million to buy Signature Funding—and we respectfully declined.

All of that happened because of our handwritten thank-you note system.

When I taught this tool to my associates, their production doubled. Closing ratios increased because, when their clients received handwritten thank-you notes, they felt a stronger connection to the loan officer—and were far less inclined to buy into the empty promises offered by the competition.

Through thank-you notes, our team members built deeper relationships with their referral partners, vendors, affiliates, and clients. Our system was so good that other mortgage companies started sending us referrals of people who wanted to be loan officers, and we would train and grow them, too.

So it's not just me. It's not just luck. The system I've created around the thank-you note works.

I still write thank-you cards every day, because each day I meet or speak with someone over the phone whom I'm grateful to get to know. My practice of writing thank-you notes—of following the strategies I'm about to teach you—has resulted not only in incredible success, but also in deeper relationships with my friends, coworkers, clients, and business associates. It's gotten me invited to exclusive parties and private events. People have a deep respect for me. They know I follow through on my commitments.

And it all started with the thank-you note.

Your Thank-You Toolkit

This book is your "thank-you toolkit."

Read it from start to finish and learn the system, from organizing your thank-you note practice to crafting a sincere message. Discover some new and creative ways to build deeper relationships with your past and current clients, along with coworkers, family, friends, and even people you've just met.

Then put your knowledge into action. Accept the Gratitude Challenges I've included for you throughout these chapters. Build your personal list of people to thank using the samples you can find at www.stevenalittlefield.com. If you have a sales team, share this system with them to make an exponential impact. Keep it nearby, and reach for it when you need a reminder to be grateful.

Within these pages are strategies and stories of successes I've had—and that others have had— from implementing this simple, reproducible, and fun system. Use the system yourself, and watch your success grow and the quality of your life and relationships expand.

You can send me a thank-you note later. I know you'll want to.

Harness Your Network

If you adopt this handwritten thank-you note system, you will not only feel happier; you'll also develop deeper, more meaningful relationships with the people you choose to surround yourself with.

With the power of the thank-you note in your back pocket, you can harness your network in ways you've never dreamed of before.

You don't need experience. You don't need much of anything to get started, except a pen, some cards, and an open heart. Rich or poor, new to an industry or old hand, up or down, you can begin this practice today. You can create the kind of life you want to lead from thin air.

I know. I'm living proof. The day they arrested me, I thought my life was over.

I had no idea that it was really just beginning.

Chapter 1

Business Is Personal

Now What?

"What're you in for, kid?"

I glanced over at the inmate across from me—an unshaven, tattooed man in his sixties who smelled like cigarettes. We were in a holding cell with a few other guys at the local San Joaquin county jail. In five days, I would be driven to the prison at Mountain View to serve my time.

I told him I'd been arrested for possession of cocaine with the intent to sell.

He gave a raspy smoker's chuckle and shook his head. "Listen, professor, if anyone asks you why you're in here, tell them you're in for murder. One of your teachers gave you a grade you didn't agree with and you stabbed him DEAD. Nobody will fuck with a crazy murderer," he said.

My first piece of advice to those seeking success is to *avoid* jail. If, like me, you end up facing jail time, my second piece of advice is to follow those instructions to the letter.

When I got to Mountain View and people asked what I was in for, I told them, "Murder. I stabbed my teacher to death. Why do you ask?"

No one bothered me.

That was December of 1984. In March, I had a court appearance, and the judge released me early for time served. They gave me four years of probation and one thousand community service hours.

I was a convicted felon. I had failed to earn my bachelor's degree. Medical school was no longer an option.

What now?

I knew I needed to find another way to be successful—but how? My uncle John was an engineer who became a really successful salesman. He'd worked his way up to become the executive vice president of Gillette Paper Mate. And the sales world didn't care that much about the felony on my record.

I decided to hone my sales skills and become a mortgage loan officer.

I signed up for every seminar that came to town. Tony Robbins, Zig Ziglar, Jim Rohn, Joe Girard, and Brian Tracy—you name it. At the breaks, I handed out and collected business cards. I was a networking maniac. But the cards piled up, and that frustrated me. I knew I was missing opportunities.

How could I possibly stand out from the crowd, if I was just one card in a mountain of others?

A Spark of Gratitude

Then, one weekend, I attended a seminar in San Jose, California, by a very successful real estate agent named Tom Hopkins.

My purpose in attending was to meet real estate agents and to learn how Tom had made it to the top. I listened and took notes diligently during the whole program. After the seminar, I reread the notebook he'd given us.

In the back were some sample thank-you card responses and scripts.

This is it, I thought. I knew I could apply this tool. I would have to rephrase some of his words, but I figured I could make it work—that I could slip these handwritten notes into my daily routine, both out of real gratitude and as a method to increase my visibility in the marketplace.

It was the answer to the question I'd been struggling with: What one thing could I do in a short period of time that would leave people with the deepest possible impression of me? That would launch me over that first hurdle in creating relationships of real value?

I got to work.

I'd collected a number of cards during the Tom Hopkins seminar, so I began with those. I wrote thank-you notes to each and every one of the contacts I had made. Then I kept going. Every time I met new people, every time I talked to them on the phone, every time I saw an article that was relevant to them, each time they did something nice or when we shared a success—another thank-you note got dropped in the mail.

At first, the task felt difficult to keep up with. I was still making sales calls on ten real estate offices a day, plus meeting people at broker caravans and networking events and interacting with everyone else I could think of, and I didn't have a system yet.

But I began to see positive results from the notes right away.

One of the agents I'd met at the Hopkins seminar, Phil—whom I'd sent a note to and followed up on with a call—granted me an appointment the following week to meet with him at his office. His office was in my territory but was a "closed" office, meaning they didn't allow loan officers into their office. You could leave your flyers at the front desk, but you couldn't talk to the Realtors unless you had an appointment. After my meeting with Phil, they let me into the office whenever I popped by, and I was able to do business with Phil and four of the five other agents in that office, resulting in an extra $2,500 a month in commissions for me—the equivalent of about $7,400 in 2016.

That did it. I became a believer in the power of the handwritten thank-you note.

You're next.

Business Is Personal

Business is personal.

This is the reason that thank-you notes are such a powerful force. There is no difference between professional relationships and personal ones. Business life and personal life are one, if you want to find success on your own terms.

When you make business personal, you attract people who inspire and energize you. You look forward to seeing and talking with them. Even if you have to deliver bad news, those conversations become much easier because of your deeper relationships. You feel grateful for and inspired by your own life.

But if you leave the "personal" out of your business dealings, that's a whole different world. Your values align less with the people around you. You wake up in the morning with a feeling of dread because you don't want to face the day, and your work ethic is a shadow of what it could be. You don't trust the people you work with. It's a miserable existence.

Making business personal is how you win the success game.

As a twenty-three-year-old mortgage loan officer just starting out, I understood that my job was to do everything in my power to be in front of a person who had the desire to borrow money and the ability to repay it. That was how I made my money. I also understood that the other part of my responsibility was to treat that individual the way I would a friend, because that's what he or she was—a friend. That was how I made my life.

You may not be in the mortgage loan business, but this same equation holds true for you. Your job is to get in front of the right people, and to treat them as you would a friend.

This chapter will teach you the secret to standing out, share the science of gratitude, show you the power of personal touch, and introduce my top five strategies for transforming your life with thank-you notes.

Stand Out

God may judge our insides, but people judge us by our appearance and our behaviors. It takes less than seven seconds for a person to form an initial opinion about us, for good or bad. And we meet a lot of people. You've probably heard the adage that the secret to success is being in the right place at the right time. So to improve your chances of success, you need to be in more places more often. That way, you can run into influential people, opportunities, and life-altering ideas just when you need them most.

But meeting influential people isn't enough. You also need them to remember you after you've met.

As a young mortgage loan officer, I went to more meet and greets, golf tournaments, church outings, and sporting events than you would think humanly possible, and

I collected more business cards than my pockets could hold. I soon figured out, however, that the goal is not just to show up everywhere, but to make an impression.

How do you stand out from the crowd?

There's no better way to amplify a first impression—or even correct it—than by showing exemplary manners, gratitude, and appreciation by following up. And when you follow up with a handwritten thank-you note, you can bet you're going to stand apart from everyone else.

Without further action and interaction on your part, you'll fade into oblivion, no matter how impressive you are during that first meeting. Saying thank you helps you stand out, every time.

The Science of Gratitude

Gratitude isn't just some airy-fairy concept invented by hippies living on mountaintops. In recent years, science has discovered some pretty impressive facts about the power that appreciation and connection have in our lives.

Stay in Touch

I was at a Dale Carnegie course on human relations when I first heard the amazing statistic that 80 percent of all sales are made after the eighth contact, and that 90 percent of all salespeople stop after the first contact.

That means that if you meet someone and send that person a handwritten thank-you note, congratulations are in order: you just made twice as many contacts as 90 percent of your competition! That immediately puts you in the top 10 percent of your colleagues.

And with the thank-you note in your corner, it gets even better.

Each time we come into contact with another person, a neural pathway is created in our brain. What happens when we meet ten people at one event? The neural pathways get crowded and confused. When an individual receives your thank-you note three days after the event, he remembers the event first, and then he remembers you. Now it's just you and your thank-you note saturating his neural pathway. Every other person he met at that event has dissolved in his mind. There is no more crowding and confusion.

You have separated yourself from the herd. He is now thinking about you with gratitude and appreciation. And he has your card in his hand, not nine others that would only dilute the connection.

Staying in touch with thank-you notes also helps you to establish trust with people. Remember, if you want to get paid for excellent service, you need to develop relationships built on trust—and trust is built over time. The thank-you note demonstrates commitment and consistency to your client, which lends you credibility. That reinforces your trustworthiness.

When people like you and trust you, guess what? They want to do business with you. And if they are not in the position to do business with you, they want to offer you someone who can.

The Law of Reciprocity

Another amazing thing that the humble thank-you note sets off is the Law of Reciprocity.

The Law of Reciprocity is a term coined by author and psychology professor Robert Cialdini. It boils down to this: when you do something nice for someone, he or she will want to do something nice for you.

Science has proven that the simple act of being grateful increases your own personal well-being. When you appreciate yourself and others, you become a little kinder, walk a little taller, and find that good things happen to you. The more gratitude you give, the more abundance you receive from the universe in an exponential way.

Thank-you notes kick off the Law of Reciprocity by getting the sense of gratitude flowing. The people receiving your handwritten thank-you note get to feel appreciated, and when they feel appreciated, they then become more abundant. Studies have shown that, when people feel appreciated, they become more giving.

And here's where human nature kicks in. When you send a note, the drive to reach out to you is triggered in the recipient, because the need to show appreciation after receiving appreciation is in our DNA. When someone does something nice for us, we want to do something nice for him or her in return.

The Hare Krishnas banked on the Law of Reciprocity. Each time a member gave a person on the street or in an airport a flower, he would ask the recipient for a donation. More often than not, he got one. The sect would not have persisted if this were not the case.

The handwritten thank-you note is even more powerful than a flower, because with it, you don't just trigger the Law of Reciprocity. You also reinforce the neural pathway in your recipient's brain and build on the relationship you laid the foundation for when you first met the person.

Thank-you notes are a simple way to selfishly pay it forward. You get to benefit, your client gets to benefit, and the universe gets to benefit because there's far more gratitude at play. Sending a thank-you note creates appreciation, which creates kindness, which creates the kind of energy that makes for a better world.

The Power of Personal Touch

Never underestimate the power of personal touch—especially in our digital age.

Some of us are old enough to appreciate the "before" and "after" of the introduction of email. Do you remember when you got your first account and started receiving messages? The technology alone was amazing, how someone could write something three thousand miles away and, almost instantly, there it would appear right in front of you.

Wow, I thought, *this is going to save so much time!*

Well, for many of us, what used to be exciting has now become daily drudgery. We receive so many emails every day that there is nothing special about them. What we once saw as a time saver has transformed us into "screen-sucking" prisoners. Emails are no longer rare, and therefore they are no longer special.

Meanwhile, when was the last time you received a hand-written card in the mail and barely read it, or threw it away immediately? Even the birthday cards from your broker or dentist get more attention than most emails. Most of the time, you read and reread that note, think good thoughts about the sender, and sometimes even save it.

Think about it. What goes through your mind when you get a handwritten note?

- I am important to this person.
- They appreciate me.
- My gift brought him/her joy.
- I am on their mind.
- They took time out of their day for me.
- They want to stay connected.

Now, don't you want your network contacts to associate you with these feelings?

When a hand-addressed card comes in the mail, people pay extra attention to it. Sometimes it's the first thing they open, and sometimes they save the best for last. Some people even wait for a time when they can sit down, uninterrupted, and give it the attention it is due before they read it. Then it sits on a desk in full view or is displayed on a wall. It is kept as a physical reminder of the time, effort, and thought that was put into it by the sender. It's a reminder of professionalism, class, and courtesy. A reminder that you are important.

Go the extra mile. Send a handwritten thank-you note to express your gratitude, instead of the typical dashed-off email.

The Five Strategies

If you want to create a tribe of loyal, fun people, a handwritten thank-you note is how you do it. Over the years, I've developed five simple strategies to supercharge the power of this tool, which I'll share with you in the following chapters: forge a gratitude mindset, get organized, write to connect, send cards for all occasions, and magnetize referrals.

Forge a gratitude mindset. Going through the motions of writing a card isn't enough. You have to mean it. I'll show you how to create a mindset that infuses your thank-you notes with the power of true gratitude.

Get organized. Even though it takes only a few minutes to write a note, we can collect dozens of cards from a single event. Those add up fast, and if you're not careful, sending thank-you notes can become a full-time job. I'll share my tricks for getting organized, so you can make the biggest impact on your clients in the least amount of time.

Write to connect. What you put in the thank-you note matters. Generic messages that pitch you and your business will only hurt you. I'll teach you how to write a note that truly connects with the person receiving it, so that he or she feels inspired to continue the relationship.

Send cards for all occasions. You can send thank-you notes after networking events and interviews—but why stop there? The more gratitude you put out into the world, the more success will come back to you. I'll pull back the curtain and reveal just how many opportunities you have to use this system in your everyday life.

Magnetize referrals. One of the most powerful effects of the thank-you note system is its ability to create an incredibly strong referral funnel for your business. I'll show you my secrets to making this dream into a reality.

The more you leverage these strategies, the more you can maximize the power of the thank-you note in your business and personal life.

Initiate Gratitude

I've made so many friends because of business. And all of those relationships started with the very same thing: me sending a handwritten thank-you note.

Sending handwritten thank-you notes is a proactive way for me to initiate gratitude. When I started doing this thirty years ago, I began attracting gratitude as well. I started doing business with people who were grateful and who wanted to do business with me.

I also collected opportunities that wouldn't have come to me any other way. And you will, too.

It all begins with a gratitude mindset.

Chapter 2

Forge a Gratitude Mindset

When the Dam Breaks

Did you see *Pale Rider* with Clint Eastwood? Remember the scene where the miners are happily panning for gold in the stream flowing by their camp, when suddenly they hear this explosion, and the water stops running because someone has dammed up the river upstream?

That was me when the financial crisis of 2008 struck.

That trillion-dollar financial meltdown blew the economy to bits and, seemingly out of nowhere, the money supply shut off. In short order, my company went from funding 350 loans a month to 8. Without the resources to support the proverbial alligator, we cleared our warehouse lines, paid our employees, and closed Signature Funding's doors.

I personally went from making $200,000 a month to making $10,000 a month. As you can imagine, that was quite a swing. It could have torn me apart.

Lucky for me, I have a pretty strong gratitude mindset.

After liquidating everything I owned, I paid cash for

a Ford Edge and became absolutely debt free. No dogs, no cats, no house, no credit cards, nada. Nothing. Zilch.

When you have no debt, you don't need much money. I moved in with my brother, David, continuing to work as a loan officer for $100,000 a year while golfing and taking frequent vacations. I traveled the world. I saw Chile, Saudi Arabia, Dubai, Ireland, Scotland, Hong Kong, Argentina, Vietnam, Italy, and Brazil. Do you know whom I stayed with along the way? All of the friends I'd built relationships with by first sending them handwritten thank-you notes.

The freedom was exhilarating. In the end, that event reminded me that success isn't just about your bank balance. It's about your ability to live life on your terms, surrounded by people you value, and who value you.

A gratitude mindset makes this kind of success possible.

The Gratitude Mindset

What is a gratitude mindset?

At its heart, a gratitude mindset is being present enough in the moment to find one thing to be grateful for. Right now, for example, the odds are good that you can see. You can hear. You can breathe. You can smell. You probably didn't sleep in a hospital last night. You have food in the fridge and a roof over your head. The list goes on and on.

With a gratitude mindset, it's natural to wake up and think, *What can I do to be happy today?*

A gratitude mindset is scientifically proven to open the door to more relationships, improve your physical and psychological health, enhance empathy, and reduce aggression. It also helps you sleep better, improves your self-esteem, and increases your mental strength, among many other benefits.

Without a gratitude mindset, we feel more anxiety, tension, stress, anger, and frustration. We feel like we never have enough, and that means we're always hungry for more. We become so focused on getting more that we always feel like we're missing out, because the mind can focus on only one thing at a time. If you're focused on what you don't have, then you can't focus on and appreciate what you do have. That's when you really miss out.

Gratitude affects all of us, whether we're aware of it or not. Imagine how you felt the last time someone didn't acknowledge a gift you sent. You probably complained to yourself or someone else about that person's ungratefulness. When we're waiting for a thank-you that doesn't come, we can't help but feel disappointed.

You don't want to be the person who forgets to thank someone for doing something nice for you. You never want to forget how good a little appreciation feels, or how easy it is to create.

With a strong gratitude mindset, we are always asking ourselves questions such as these: Whom can I send a thank-you note to today? Whom can I touch today? Whom can

I show my appreciation to, and for what? Then we actually go and send it.

We're not put on this earth simply to acquire wealth—to work ourselves into the ground and sacrifice the here and now in the name of prestige and material trappings. We're here to connect, to bond with others, and to create our own tribe. The first step in that direction is forging a powerful gratitude mindset.

This chapter will show you why sending thank-you notes is a joy instead of a chore, help you overcome your objections to writing notes, and guide you in making initial connections with people that open the door for you to send your notes later.

"I Get to Send Out Cards Later"

The most important mindset shift you can make is going from "I have to send out cards later" to "I get to send out cards later."

You might wonder, why does it matter? The cards are going out one way or another, aren't they? Who cares how I feel when I write them?

It matters because your attitude finds its way into what you're doing.

Think about it. When your colleague, assistant, or children hear you complain about the act of writing a thank-you card as a task, what message are you sending? The next time your assistant receives a card from you, he or she will only imagine what a chore it was for you to write it, rather than accepting it as a sincere gesture of appreciation.

Your mindset affects what you write in the card, too. As I said in the last chapter, using a personal touch matters. The generic "I enjoyed meeting you last week. Please keep me in mind for your banking needs" does more harm to your reputation than sending nothing at all. The visual I get when I receive such a card is that of someone going through the motions at his or her desk, chained to the Thank-You Card Assembly Line, wishing he or she were anywhere but there.

But if you approach your thank-you notes with genuine gratitude, that shines through. What used to be an obligation is now an opportunity—and people will feel it. You'll start reaping the rewards of positive feedback as well as increased sales. You'll no longer look at this as a task to check off your to-do list. You might even start seeking out new opportunities to write notes because you enjoy it so much.

When that happens, you're well on your way to a strong gratitude mindset.

Overcome Your Own Objections

If you've been in any type of sales position in the last fifty years, you understand that you've got to be prepared to overcome the customer's objections, no matter how seemingly ridiculous they may be.

Well, now you're the one on the other side of the sales table, and you've got to talk yourself around all the excuses you might have for not writing thank-you notes. Here are a few of my personal favorites:

I'm too busy

It takes only two minutes to write a card. If you use the tactics I share with you in chapter 3 to get organized—such as using dead time, setting goals, tracking your progress, and eliminating distractions—you will be able to fit the habit of writing thank-you notes seamlessly into your day.

Slow and steady wins the race. Don't forget that.

Handwritten notes are a dying breed

Handwritten notes *are* rare—which makes them special, which in turn makes you stand out from the pack.

When something is unique and rare, doesn't that make it more precious? And I can personally vouch that they aren't extinct. Just because you're not receiving any doesn't mean they're not being sent. Start sending some yourself, and you might be pleasantly surprised by what you start receiving in return. Sending positive energy out brings positive energy back in to you.

By sending a note instead of an email, you'll likely get more attention from the reader at a time when it's convenient, rather than a little attention instantaneously, when it's inconvenient. Your client is receiving the gift of your attention. You give of yourself when you handwrite your message.

I don't have good stationery—and I don't want to spend a lot of money

The simpler the stationery, the better. No need to have monograms or linen stock. You don't want to be cheap, but you also don't want to be over the top.

If a packet of twelve cards and envelopes costs you less than a couple of movie tickets or two trips to the coffee shop, and it has the potential to lead to more business and greater connections, the decision should be a simple one to make.

I don't know what to say

I'll be sharing plenty of templates for what to say in later chapters. But even without those, if all else fails, why not try "please" and "thank you"?

What would you say to this person if he or she were sitting next to you? Your voice is your voice, whether in person or on paper. If you write what you would have said, you are being genuine.

If you're still not sure what to say, practice before you start writing. Create the message on your computer first. Some people compose better when they're not restricted by their penmanship. Using the computer first can also catch spelling and grammar errors before you put pen to paper. Just don't let this trick stifle or hinder you from being spontaneous and writing a note when you don't have the convenience of a computer.

Learning what to say is just like learning anything else: the more you practice, the easier it will become.

My handwriting is awful

My handwriting isn't the best either. Take it from me: the recipient will cut you some slack. After all, you made the effort.

Elementary penmanship is not the standard by which your thoughtfulness will be judged. That said, neatness does count when it comes to writing legible notes. Also, do not cross out more than one word per card; it's best not to cross out any at all. Again, this is where a rough draft created on the computer with spell check can be a useful habit.

Notes are for women

Real men do write notes. I happen to be one of them.

Intelligent, savvy men know the power of the handwritten note. They've experienced abundance both professionally and personally as a result of sending notes. They've also been impressed and inspired by others from whom the have received notes. Regardless of your political affiliation, you can appreciate that former presidents Reagan, Carter, Clinton, George H., and George W. Bush were all known to write handwritten notes.

Being thoughtful is not gender specific. Consider this: a thoughtful male executive is seen as unique, whereas a thoughtful female executive is the norm. Gentlemen, don't you want to stand out and be noticed?

I won't have a record of what I sent

Minor detail. If you've written a rough draft, keep the draft. Make a photocopy of the note and file it, or scan it and keep it in your contacts or email list, if you have to. Not having a record should never stop you from sending a note.

The note will take too long to get there

Sometimes you need to thank someone right away, such as right after a job interview. You don't want too much time to lapse from when you meet the interviewer and when you thank him or her.

In that case, you can send a detailed thank-you email to the interviewer right away, and then send the card to arrive within forty-eight hours. Or you can hand deliver the note and leave it with the receptionist. Either way, don't talk yourself out of sending the note.

I forgot to send it and now it's too late

Again, don't let this keep you from sending it. And don't start the note with an apology (such as "Forgive me for the delay . . ."). Instead, say what you originally intended to say, and then finish with a brief apology without making a big deal out of it. This approach is genuine, sincere, and thoughtful. What more could anyone ask for?

Connect with Gratitude

Now that you've gotten yourself over the mental hurdle of sending thank-you notes, whom are you going to send them to? This is where a gratitude mindset can really up your game: by helping you make powerful initial connections.

When you make a connection with someone, don't just chat about the weather. Have a real conversation with people you meet. Be grateful that you've encountered this person, and show genuine curiosity in him or her. This is how you'll spot kindred spirits—people you can help and who can also add value to your life.

(By the way, this is also the time to make sure you get people's contact information. Make sure you have their mailing address. If it's not on their card, have them write it down for you, or verify the address you've recorded and make the necessary changes. If you're uncomfortable asking for an address, don't worry; it's not as hard as you think. Just tell them you want it so you can send them your card, or say, "If I wanted to send you something in the mail, which address would be best?" I've never had anyone balk at giving me their address.)

Without a gratitude mindset, you might become one of the skeptics who meet someone and think, "I doubt I will ever do business with this guy, so why am I bothering? Sure, I'll send this first card out, but I probably won't hear back, so I'll just go through the motions."

Thinking that way just sabotages your efforts. When you meet someone for the first time, you have no idea where that relationship might take you, personally or professionally.

It's easy to look back at close friendships, successful partnerships, or lucrative referrals and be grateful for those connections. How do you feel when you think of that person? What emotions come up when you look back at the time you've spent together, or the deals and negotiations you entered into together?

Seriously, think about it right now. Do you feel energized, excited, and proud?

Now, instead of looking back, change your perception and try looking forward. Each time you make an initial connection, be grateful from the start. Feel those same emotions of pride, excitement, and energy, right now. In that frame of mind, write out your thank-you note.

You have no idea where that introduction may lead. But

with the positive energy and feelings you have, don't the possibilities seem endless?

Choose Wisely

With the thank-you note system, you'll make more connections than you ever have before. But that doesn't mean you need to keep all of them.

As I said earlier, business is personal, and I've had to learn to be mindful of whom I choose to develop relationships with. Because my intention is to turn business associates into friends, I've sought out those who meet my "Red Velvet Rope" policy, a term coined by *New York Times* bestselling author Michael Port in his book *Book Yourself Solid*. The essence of the policy is this: there are some people we are meant to serve, and some people, not so much.

The people I've chosen to work with share my values, work ethic, personality type, and interests, as well as hobbies and characteristics that are important to me. Those who don't, I've walked on by.

You can make anyone your friend with this system I'm teaching you, because the handwritten note is a powerful tool. You too will want to be thoughtful as to whom you bring into your tribe with it.

Personal Business Is Fun Business

When you have a gratitude mindset, business isn't just personal. It's also fun.

My first boss, Clay, had a ski boat. One day, after his wife had blown out the engine of their Blazer, he asked me to tow the thing with my truck, which I did. On the way back from the marina, he invited me up to his house for lunch with his family. He so appreciated the favor and the way I interacted with his family that he told me to invite a couple of real estate agents to meet up with us on a Friday afternoon to water ski.

I was grateful. And I chose to invite two agents who were friendly but still hadn't committed to working with me.

We picked our agents up at the dock, and the six of us skied and drank for hours. In the evening, we dropped the agents back off at the dock, grabbed a bite to eat, and then headed out to the delta to camp on one of the islands. The next morning, we skied our way back into breakfast on a sheet of smooth glass. It was a fabulous way to spend the weekend.

On Monday, I had messages from my agents saying that they had clients they wanted me to prequalify.

How do you like that? Go skiing on Friday, get clients on Monday. This was a great marketing plan, one that we implemented every weekend that we could. By the end of that year, I was making twice what my brothers made, and more money than my father made as a physician. I had really worked only seven months—and most of my work involved hanging out with people I really liked and enjoying life.

This is how I continue to live, to this day: surrounded by fun people who need or want what I have to offer.

You build your tribe of like-minded, fun individuals by spotting those you'd like to do business with. Then you differentiate yourself from the herd with the handwritten thank-you note. It really is that simple.

But guess what? It gets even simpler. In the next chapter, I'll show you how to organize your thank-you note system so that you can not only make powerful impressions on people; you can also do it fast.

Gratitude Challenge

List five people who inspire you to be more grateful in life. Send each of them a handwritten thank-you note.

1. _____

2. _____

3. _____

4. _____

5. _____

Chapter 3

Get Organized

The Big Picture

We all have good intentions of writing out thank-you notes after a networking event or party . . . until we clean out our pockets, purses, and briefcases and find that the corner of our desk has an unyielding mound of business cards on it.

Most of them we don't even remember getting, let alone do we recall any specific details about the individual or conversation that took place when that card came into our hands. Was it a referral, sent to us by someone else? Or did we actually meet this person?

So we put it off. We figure we'll tackle the issue of what to do with the card later, or eventually hire someone else to organize them.

Needless to say, the stack continues to grow. Now we don't want to send out notes because we are embarrassed about how much time has lapsed since we first met these potential business contacts.

This is how it goes, event after event, lead after lead going down the drain. Until you get organized.

The Long Game

That pile of business cards is no different from any of the other piles in our lives (the "to be filed" pile, the tax receipts pile, the laundry pile, and the list goes on). The longer you put it off, the harder it will be and the longer it will take to deal with when you finally get around to it.

That's why it's critical to stay organized when it comes to sending thank-you notes.

By having a system in place, no matter where you go or whom you meet, you'll be ahead of everyone else because you do one thing that they don't: *follow up*. While everyone else is too distracted to keep in touch, there you are, scooping up the rewards.

Without a system in place, you become one of the nameless masses, missing out on half of the opportunities that come your way—if not more.

When it comes to getting organized, the key thing to remember is that you're in this for the long game. Slow and steady wins the race. Doing just a few notes every day or every week makes what you thought was a chore into a peaceful way to spend a few minutes of your day.

Once you make note writing a habit, it will become something you look forward to doing. Following my system, it takes only about two minutes to write a card, and the feeling of appreciation you have when expressing your gratitude will last even longer.

We're going to get into more details about when to send a handwritten thank-you note and what to actually write in it in the next chapter. But for now, let's take a step back and examine the actual system you will need to employ to handle the volume of valuable contacts that will now be coming your way. Because if you do what I tell you to do, you'll have more contacts than you ever thought possible.

The System

I've broken down my system for organizing thank-you cards into a step-by-step cheat sheet. If you follow this path, you'll be able to create heartfelt connections in a manageable manner from day one.

> *Step 1: Address the envelopes.* Take a contact's business card from your pile, address the envelope, and then repeat with the rest of the cards until complete. Address all of the envelopes at one time. (If you're using a self-inking return address stamp, this is the time to stamp the envelope, too.) Having all of your envelopes addressed and sitting on your desk is like a live to-do list, reminding you to write one by one until you are done.

Note: You might leverage your time by having an assistant address the envelopes for you after a major event or party that leaves you with a huge volume of cards to attend to. (For me, this also helps to make sure they get to the appropriate location, as my handwriting is not the most legible.) Unless the volume is too massive to handle on your own, however, it's better to address the envelopes yourself, because as we've seen, the personal touch makes a real difference.

Step 2: Write the cards. Take a note card and write it out, remembering something from the conversation you had with the person you're writing to. Fold the card in half and place it in the envelope, fold down. Repeat with the rest of the cards until complete. *Do not seal the envelopes!*

Note: Writing on the card is the only part of this process that requires you to think. Don't worry, I'll provide you with some basic phrases and templates for several situations in the next few chapters.

Step 3: Add your business cards. This is my secret weapon. I found that when I was at mixers and networking functions, everyone was handing out their cards, hoping that others would contact them. I didn't want my card shuffled into the deck with everybody else's, so I quit passing cards out and became a collector of business cards instead.

Put two or three business cards in each envelope, and repeat until complete. This is the best way to differentiate your card from all of the others your recipient collected during a networking event.

Step 4: Seal the envelopes. Go through your finished stack of cards and seal each envelope. Repeat until complete. (Note: this activity can be delegated to an assistant.)

Step 5: Stamp the envelopes. Once all the envelopes are sealed, add a real stamp to each one of them; don't use the postal meter in your office. We all want to feel like we're one of a kind, not mass produced on an assembly line. Repeat until complete. (This activity can also be delegated to an assistant.)

Step 6: Mail the notes. The handwritten thank-you note: easy to send, easy to forget to mail. When your stack is finished, remember to drop the envelopes in the mailbox.

Once I implemented this system, I was able to send fifteen-plus thank-you notes a day—spending just half an hour per day on them—and that's when my business really started taking off.

But you don't have to stop here. You can go even deeper.

Go Deeper

During the course of your conversations, you will likely identify the individuals you would like to form a deeper relationship with—people who strike you as especially fun, energizing, inspiring, and mutually beneficial. Send a thank-you note to everyone, sure, but for these select individuals, you'll want to do more to bridge the gap.

A thank-you note opens the door to possibilities. But this one extra step is a game changer.

> ***Step 7: Follow up by phone.*** Once you've identified the people you want to build a deeper relationship with, follow up with them by phone. Make a phone call to each of your select individuals three days after you mail their thank-you note, or when you're sure they have received it. If the person is local, invite the recipient to meet for a coffee.

Going deeper by following up with a call gives you an opportunity to revisit the conversation you had when you initially met your new contacts. It allows you to find out if there is a way for you to provide value to them, or if they can benefit you in some way. Use this opportunity to set an appointment, either to meet or to call back in the future.

When you do this, the possibilities open right up.

Pro Tips

The step-by-step system will go a long way toward making you a Jedi master of the thank-you card. Even so, there are a few pro tips you can try to make the experience even more efficient. These include getting organized, using dead time, setting goals, and tracking your progress.

Get Organized

Before you attend a big networking event or even just before you leave your office on Friday afternoon, put a stack of blank cards and envelopes along with stamps on the corner of your desk. This will be a visual reminder for you that you need to write your cards—not to mention very convenient. Doing this will also help you create a habit that you can stick to.

Use Dead Time

Plan to write the cards out when you first come back from lunch every day, or when you have a few minutes before a meeting but you don't want to start on a large work project. I often use the time that I am on hold on the telephone to address the envelopes and write out the message.

Some executives make writing notes their first priority when they get in to work, while enjoying a cup of coffee or settling in for the day. Others make it the last thing they do before they leave. Either way, you might see how starting or ending your day in gratitude is a habit worth keeping.

Keep a stack of cards in your trunk or briefcase that you can use while you're waiting for appointments and meetings to start. Rather than frantically texting or typing out an email in a nice restaurant and interrupting someone else's dining experience, quietly take pen to paper and write out those cards. The addresses are in your contacts list anyway. There is no excuse why you can't get them done, stamped, and mailed while you wait.

Set Goals

If you can put a time constraint on how soon you want to mail out a card after meeting someone, you'll send a lot more cards out, a lot faster. For example, you might set a goal to have the card mailed out within forty-eight to seventy-two hours of making a person's acquaintance.

If you do this, it will help to write the date that you met the person on the back of the card, when you get it. While you're at it, you can also make a specific note about your contact him- or herself on the card, which will help you later when you're crafting your message.

Track Your Progress

You can also keep track of the thank-you cards you send. If you can track something, you can manage it, and this is absolutely true of your gratitude practice. Creating a list of whom you've sent a note to reinforces your subconscious mind to continue the practice. (So do the positive reactions you get from sending the notes themselves, by the way.) It also gives you a sense of personal accomplishment.

If you know you will not have time to immediately enter someone's information into your contact management system when you send a card, however, don't despair. You can just write yourself a note (preferably on the contact's card) that you mailed this person a thank-you card as a reference point for later. It could be something as simple as "TY 1/20," which could mean you sent a thank-you on January 20.

A Note on Card Style

One place where people sometimes get hung up on sending thank-you notes is with choosing a card style.

As I said in chapter 2, the simpler the stationery, the better. The most expensive cards usually don't make you look good; they make you look arrogant and ostentatious.

Blank cards are best. You should not need the prompt of "thank you" prewritten on the card. Staying gender neutral is also a good idea. Try to incorporate your style with a design or color that represents you. Buy a box or two of Papyrus or Crane-style cards and small stationery pages that have classic trim. You may also want to look into cards that are more personalized with your initials or monogram incorporated on the front or in the border. Your company logo works just fine, too.

Set Yourself Apart

Use a card that reflects the signature color associated with your brand.

- Have personalized stationery produced for you.

- Find a local printer that can create customized note cards and envelopes for you. Then send that local printer a handwritten thank-you note to convert him or her into a friend and referral source.

What can you comfortably afford? Nice paper makes the experience of writing that much richer and more enjoyable. If you have it, you'll take a little extra time and effort to present yourself in the best possible light, and that will only ever work in your favor. Why waste good paper on cheap words?

A friend of mine, Lisa, used a very creative way to notify her friends and family about her new mailing address when she bought her first home. They were so supportive of her during her frantic home-buying experience that she wanted to do more than send out a blast email.

So she cut up moving boxes into rectangular shapes that fit into a traditional business envelope. With a black marker, she wrote, "Still living out of boxes! Here's my new address . . ." For the people who'd sent her gift cards to congratulate her, she wrote, "Still living out of boxes and on my way to Home Depot—AGAIN! Thank you so much for your generous donation to my fixer-upper. Here's my new address."

Lisa heard from everyone about how creative her card was. And because it was made of bulky, corrugated box material, the envelope had such a unique feel to it that people opened her mail first. The cardboard was also less likely to get lost in piles of mail and papers on their desks until they could update their address book.

Make people feel special but also comfortable with your stationery. This is an opportunity to show how much you care, not how much you have.

Gratitude, in Short Order

How many times have you gone to a meet and greet, party, church, or some sporting event and met someone you really enjoyed? Maybe you got his business card, or logged his phone number into your phone. And then a day went by.

Then a week. Then you completely forgot about reaching out to him altogether.

Once you have a system to keep in touch, that scenario falls off your radar. It just stops happening. Instead, you find yourself with an influx of wonderful, exciting people. All because you took a short moment to send a little gratitude their way.

With a practical system in place that's ready to handle as many thank-you cards as you can throw at it, there's only one thing left to do: write the notes. In the next chapter, I'll show you how to make a powerful connection with people using thank-you notes.

Gratitude Challenge

List five people who make your life easier or more organized. Send each of them a handwritten thank-you note.

1. _____

2. _____

3. _____

4. _____

5. _____

Chapter 4

Write to Connect

Early Thank-You Training

I was fortunate enough to be raised to write thank-you cards at an early age. Granted, I didn't see myself as "fortunate" at the time.

As a kid, I cursed the day after my birthday or Christmas, when my mother would sit me down at the table, plunk a stack of envelopes and cards in front of me, and supervise my "appreciation" for my gifts as if I were being monitored during a standardized test. It felt like a chore . . . but I did get better at it as time went by.

I remembered to not only include the "thank you" part of the message, but also mention the specific gift and how I was looking forward to using it, playing with it, or wearing it. The responses I received from the gift-givers were great.

Better yet, I noticed that the gifts got better and better as my notes of appreciation grew more refined.

For example, one year, I got a giraffe stuffed animal from my aunt. I wrote her a note thanking her for the giraffe and telling her how it filled out my safari collection. "Now I'm working on my sea-animal collection," I added. For Christmas, she sent me a giant stuffed Shamu whale. I was pretty excited, and she was happy knowing that I loved my gifts.

That's what happens when your thank-you note truly connects with someone.

Words That Connect

A thank-you note isn't just a lifeless piece of mail. It's a spark of living gratitude, passed from your hands into the hands and heart of the person who receives it.

Research tells us that the number-one emotion people crave is to feel appreciated. When you invest the time to really connect with someone, you are saying, "I see you. I hear you. And I appreciate you." The famous saying that "people don't care how much you know until they know how much you care" is absolutely true. And a handwritten thank-you note that truly connects with someone is a simple, powerful way to show how much you care.

Every time you don't make a real connection through your note, you miss an opportunity to build a deeper, more meaningful relationship with someone. And your recipient isn't the only one who suffers the consequences of that. People who go through life without making real connections are almost always unhappy. You don't even have to ask them how they feel. The misery shows on their faces and in their body postures.

That's not the life you want. And when you learn to write sincere thank-you notes, it's a far cry from the joy-filled, abundant life you'll have.

Writing personalized thank-you notes that truly connect with people gets easier with practice. But that doesn't mean I can't give you a head start.

This chapter will show you the four key things your message should do, break down the different parts of a thank-you note, and share some basic templates that you can use to get started.

The Fantastic Four

No matter whom your note is for or why you're writing it, your message should always do four things. I call these the "fantastic four" aspects of a great thank-you note: express genuine feeling, remind the reader where you met, mention something of interest, and create a call to action.

One: Express genuine feeling toward the person

You always want to open your note with a sense of honest feeling. When you do this, the message you are already sending to your recipient is, "I see you, I am grateful to have met you, and I appreciate you." That makes me feel good just writing it, and you can bet it feels good to read, too. A warm first sentiment opens people's hearts, souls, and minds to you.

Here are a few phrases that I like to use:

- *It was a pleasure to meet you . . .*
- *I enjoyed your presentation on . . .*
- *What a nice surprise to see you again at . . .*
- *I am so glad that Joe recommended you . . .*
- *So happy to hear your good news . . .*
- *Congratulations on your much-deserved promotion! It was an outstanding accomplishment, and this is only the beginning of a journey to bigger and better things . . .*

Two: Remind the reader where and how you met (if necessary)

Next, your note should remind the reader where and how you met, if necessary. You'll want to include this when you meet someone for the first time. We are bombarded by hundreds of stimuli a day, and our brains are set up to warn us against things or people who are unfamiliar. However, if you make it easy for your reader to remember you by mentioning when and where you met, that lights up the positive neural pathways in the person's brain. "Oh yeah," he or she thinks, "I remember this guy. Wow, he sent me a card. What a thoughtful person. I need to stay in touch with him."

A few examples of "when and where" phrases include the following:

- *. . . at the technology conference on Thursday.*
- *. . . during the benefit dinner for . . .*
- *. . . Joe introduced us and suggested that we connect.*

Three: Mention something you discussed or that is of interest to the reader

This is where personalization comes in. Personalization reinforces the "I see you, I hear you, and I am grateful to have met you" message. When someone receives your card and it mentions that person's child's recital or summer camp, the brain neurons start firing off endorphins: "Wow, he heard me. He actually listened to me."

These are the intangibles that people buy. You can't advertise that you're a good listener, or that you follow through with your commitments, or that you have great attention to detail. You have to demonstrate it—and a handwritten thank-you note is a perfect way to show someone all of those things and more.

Here are some examples of personalization phrases:

- *How was your trip to the mountains?*
- *I hope your move went smoothly.*

- *How is the dog training going?*
- *Did you enjoy the concert?*

Four: Create a suggestive call to action (if appropriate)

Finally, in most cases, your card should include a call to action. Sometimes it is okay to say, "I was just thinking about you." However, if you do have a call to action, make sure that it is appropriate and relevant. Remember, this is a relationship-building system, not a sales con. Your call to action could be as simple as "Let's meet for a drink to catch up," or else just a reminder that you are here to serve their needs or those of their friends. Here are a few calls to action that I use:

- *I look forward to hearing from you soon.*
- *I will follow up with you next week unless I hear from you first.*
- *How does your schedule look for coffee next week?*
- *I would love to discuss how I can best support you (we can support each other) over lunch in the next couple of weeks.*

Nuances will vary. But if your thank-you note accomplishes these four things, you know you're off to a solid start.

Parts of a Thank-You Note

Now that you know the "fantastic four" mainstays of a great thank-you note, we're ready to get into the nitty gritty of what it includes—inside and out. The seven key parts of a thank-you note are the salutation, the content, the final thought, the closing, your signature, enclosures, and the envelope.

The Salutation

Always remember to include the date in the right-hand corner. After that, you begin with the salutation. As a rule, I like to stick with the basics for this:

- Dear . . .

The name you write after that depends on the degree of formality. Use the person's full first name unless you are casual or it has already been established as acceptable to do otherwise (e.g., Christopher, Chris).

Content

Your content should always be clear and to the point. Here are a few tips:

- Do not waste time or space with introductory phrases such as "I am writing to say . . ."

- Start with "Thank you" or lead into it with sincere emotion: "What a great lunch . . ." "You were so generous to . . ."

- Stay away from negative modifiers ("I have never heard such a funny story . . ."). Rather, say, "That was an extremely funny story . . ." Or instead of "That meal was awfully good . . ." say, "Dinner was wonderful . . ."

Final Thought

You want your final thought to bring the message to a nice, natural close that inspires the reader to take action. Here are two strategies:

- Finish with an action or recap: "I look forward to connecting with you next week . . ." or "Thank you again . . ."

- Don't always ask for business. Instead, you can offer to broker a relationship for them. "I am often out networking in San Diego, so if you have a particular need for a service or product, please do not hesitate to contact me as I would be happy to make an introduction for you."

Closing

You should indent your closing to the middle of the line. Which type of close you use depends on the formality of the card. Here are some examples in each category:

- Formal: Sincerely; With best regards
- Casual: Yours truly; Regards
- Very personal: Fondly; Affectionately

Signature

The rule of thumb with the signature is that if your salutation is only a first name, you should sign only your first name. This will be the case most of the time.

Enclosures

It's also a good idea to include things with your note. For example:

- Your business card! I mentioned the power of this strategy in the last chapter. Include your business card whenever you get the chance. It is much easier for people to refer you business if they can simply hand one of your "extra" cards to a colleague. I encourage you to send two or three cards with your note instead one for this reason.

- You can sometimes also include a newspaper or magazine article. When you do, unless it is relevant to send the original (award notification, etc.), make a nice clean photocopy of it so that the recipient does not have to deal with newspaper print or see an inappropriate advertisement on the back.

The envelope

If you've taken the time to handwrite the note, don't take a shortcut by using a label or typing the envelope. Even though I've lived in San Diego most of my life, I still wouldn't wear flip-flops with my best business suit. Don't cheapen the look or feel of your note. How long does it really take to address an envelope? And remember: use real postage stamps.

Pay attention to the details when you write your notes. Following these simple instructions will allow you to write with polish, warmth, and poise.

The Basic Templates

I've learned by trial and error what to say in a thank-you note—what reactions come with certain messages. As you grow more comfortable writing these notes, you'll find a way to express yourself that's unique to you. But in the meantime, I'd like to share a little cheat sheet with you.

Here are some basic templates that you can use to get

you started. I call these my "anytime," "deeper relationship," and "thanks anyway" templates.

The "Anytime" Template

The "anytime" template can be used almost any time you meet someone. It goes like this:

Dear _____,

It was a pleasure meeting you at _____. I look forward to following up with you about _____. If you have any questions or know someone I can serve, feel free to call me.

Sincerely,

The "Deeper Relationship" Template

The "deeper relationship" template is a message you can use after you've phoned someone you want to build an even deeper relationship with.

Dear _____,

Thank you for talking to me on the telephone. I look forward to meeting with you on [date], at [location]. If you have any questions or know someone I can serve, feel free to call me.

Sincerely,

The "Thanks Anyway" Template

Every time a potential client either was declined for a loan or decided to work with someone else, I always wrote him or her a note along the lines of the "thanks anyway" template.

Dear _____,

Thank you for giving me the opportunity to work with you. I regret that I was unable to meet your needs at this time. In today's business world things change, and if anything changes for you, feel free to give me a call.

Regards,

The response from this one note alone was overwhelmingly positive. The recipients would call or send thank-you notes in return, claiming that they had never been reached out to like that after a less-than-positive outcome in a transaction.

I always explained that I was grateful to have the opportunity to work with them, that they were my priority, and it was just unfortunate that some things were and are out of my control. They always thanked me for letting them know they could count on me. Many times, when they found out the "other offer" didn't pan out, they would call me back and give me the business. Other times, they would refer business to me, simply because they felt grateful.

You can't go wrong with gratitude.

Pro Tips

Just like with the thank-you card system itself, over the years I've discovered a few pro tips that can help you connect with people at a higher level through your thank-you notes. These tips include staying present, meaning what you say, and being concise.

Stay Present

Remain in the moment while you are writing. Do not think about the stack on your desk, or you will rush your message and forget to make it unique and personal. Forget the distractions and put yourself into it. The more you can do this, the more impactful your notes will be.

Mean What You Say

Always be authentic when you're writing your notes. You have to mean what you say. For example, don't compliment something that you don't like, or say you agree with something that you don't actually agree with. If you fake it, that shows through.

What you put out into the universe comes back to you, magnified and multiplied. If you put out fallacies, you will receive them in return. Choose to send out authentic gratitude, and allow *that* to come back to you magnified and multiplied a thousandfold, instead.

Be Concise

Here's a piece of good news: a handwritten note gives you the opportunity to eliminate the ums, uhs, and ers from your speech. Now that you have a chance to think before you speak, you'll be less likely to write in circles or be chatty. And the more succinct your message is, the bigger punch it will pack.

The sheer space limitation of a note forces you to be concise. Take advantage of this, rather than seeing it as an obstacle. Remember when you start that you'll probably have space for only three sentences. What are the most important things you want to say?

Ask yourself if your message is sincere, generous, succinct, personal, and specific. If you can answer "yes" to all of these, you have succeeded!

Keep Connecting

When you write to connect, you're harnessing more than words. You're tapping into the power of real gratitude.

For some people, words flow more easily from a keyboard. For others, it happens best through handwritten journaling. Whatever your method, use it to create a rough draft. You may benefit from creating several versions of sincere notes so that when you are short on time, you can expedite the process by using your own words that you already created.

Just make sure you send it. Because it will make all the difference in the world.

Now you understand the fundamentals of what makes a strong, personalized thank-you note. But where else can you harness this superpower, apart from networking events? In chapter 5, I'll introduce you to a range of places where you can put your thank-you-writing skills to good use.

Gratitude Challenge

List five people you have a deep, valuable connection with. Send each of them a handwritten thank-you note.

1. _____

2. _____

3. _____

4. _____

5. _____

Send Notes for All Occasions

The Provost's Good Word

One of my friends recently told me about a conversation she'd had with her niece, Ana, who is a freshman away from home at college. Ana had won a few scholarships and grants to help with her tuition.

After she received the grants, her mother reminded her to send handwritten thank-you notes to the appropriate people.

One of these notes went to the provost of the university. Apparently, he doesn't get all that many handwritten thank-you cards from students. So he contacted Ana to thank her for reaching out to him that way.

"How are you enjoying school?" he asked her.

"I love it!" Ana told him honestly. In the course of the conversation, she also mentioned that all of the money she had made the previous summer was going fast, and that she was eagerly looking for work that was within walking distance of the school.

The provost was so impressed with her spirited honesty and her maturity in sending the note that he helped her find a job. He put in a good word for her at the rock-climbing facility on campus—one she had frequented since starting school.

Ana got a dream job doing what she already loved to do, and it fit into her school schedule.

"Mom was right all of those years when she told me how important thank-you notes were," Ana admitted to her aunt.

What a great lesson to learn at the ripe old age of eighteen.

When to Send a Note

Now, be honest: Did you even consider writing a thank-you note to the provost of your university, if you went?

We all recognize the opportunity to send thank-you notes after a networking event—but why stop there? Why limit the power of the system? When you find as many reasons as possible to send thank-you notes, your opportunities to create more meaningful relationships grow exponentially. The more opportunities you have, the more your business will grow. And the more meaningful relationships you surround yourself with, the richer your life will become, and the happier you will be.

I've experienced this firsthand.

Over the years, I developed the habit of sending thank-notes for almost every simple interaction I had with people. I sent folks thank-you notes for taking the time to talk with me on the telephone, thank-you notes for giving me a chance to do business together, thank-you notes for when we had a successful transaction. I sent a note when someone met with me at an open house or chatted with me at an event. And most importantly, I sent a thank-you note when I didn't get the business from the recipient. Just to name a few.

Sure enough, my dry cleaners take better care of my clothes and give me hugs every time I stop in. When I go to restaurants, my servers remember me and give me high fives, along with good tables. Many times, these friends also refer business to me. The gratitude that you put out into the world returns to you in joy and abundance, every time.

Whether you've just met a person or are seeing someone again after some time has passed, sending a note solidifies your interest in establishing or enhancing a relationship.

The more opportunities you capture to send a thank-you note, the sooner you'll be on your way to creating the business and life you intend to have for yourself.

You'll want to think of this chapter as one great big cheat sheet. We'll start with thank-you note templates for networking events and interviews, because those are both big-ticket items in the thank-you note world. Then I'll give you a full breakdown of notes you can use for any occasion—even some you probably haven't thought of yet.

Nail Your Networking Events

Networking events are the most common place to collect cards, so that you can send thank-you notes out to the people you meet later.

When you're at a networking event, mixer, or party, carry a pen with you. Then, every time you get someone's card, write notes on the back so you can remember what you talked about. What was the person interested in? Doing this gives you something meaningful to say when you sit down to write your note later.

Here are a few of my favorite thank-you note templates for networking events:

Dear _____,

It was a pleasure meeting you at the _____ event this weekend. I appreciated your presentation on _____. Can we schedule some time to talk on the phone to go over your ideas?

Dear _____,

I appreciate you sharing your story about _____ at the _____ conference on Saturday. Can you let me know when would be a good time to call you?

Dear _____,

Thank you for visiting with me at the _____ live event. I appreciate the time we shared. When can we follow up to continue our conversation about _____?

Own Your Interviews

When it comes to interviews, a handwritten thank-you note will make a lasting impression and set you apart from the competition. The reason is simple: it implies that you will always bring a bit more to your work than is expected.

To write a knock-out thank-you note after an interview, start by picking two or three specific skills you have that pair up with the needs of the organization, as you learned from the interview. Then compose a brief, handwritten thank-you note on nice stationery. Note that this is not the time to skimp on paper quality or use typed form letters.

For interviews more than any other occasion, I would advise practicing the body of the note on a separate sheet of paper. If you create better on your computer, type out the draft there.

Once you have it as succinct as possible, write it out in your handwriting or printing on the good stationery. This should eliminate any cross outs, misspellings, and fragmented or run-on sentences. If you do make a mistake, don't try to fix it. Rip that draft up, toss it, and start a new one.

Keep in mind that although you are sending a personal thank-you note, you should be respectfully professional when you address your interviewer. It's always easier to recover your bearings with that person if you overdress (being a little too stiff and impersonal) than it is if you dress down (being a little sloppy or overly familiar). Save the shorts and flip-flops for later on. For now, err on the side of overdressing.

Here are my pro tips for post-interview thank-you notes:

- Be cordial, but not too formal or serious.

- Personalize it. Don't make it read as though one company is writing to another company. Use the first and second person (I and you) as if you were carrying on a conversation, not a sales presentation/pitch.

- Use *your* voice. It should sound like you—graceful and polished.

- Avoid expressions such as "I am in receipt of" or "proposal to be sent under separate cover." Even though you want to be respectfully professional, this isn't a legal document. The message is still "I see you, I hear you, and I appreciate you."

- Spelling and grammar are important. Don't write a card the same way you would text someone or send a brief email.

A former colleague of mine, Christine, once interviewed at a prominent company where she spent more than six hours going through the "gauntlet" of seven interviewers, back to back, in a single afternoon.

When she finally got home, she sat down and wrote each of those seven people a thank-you note on her Crane cards, making sure to spell all the names correctly using the business cards she had collected. She sent them out the next day.

When Christine went back for a couple of follow-up interviews, she was pleased to see that her notes were still on the desks or sideboards of the recipients. And yes, not only was she offered a job, but a higher executive position was actually created just for her, because they felt that what they were lacking within her department was her kind of leadership and professionalism.

Christine's follow-up and attention to making others feel appreciated earned her the right reputation even before her first day. If you follow her lead, you'll experience the same thing.

I've composed a few interview templates to get you started.

Dear _____,

Thank you for meeting with me regarding the _____ position. I look forward to hearing from you about our next steps.

Dear _____,

Thank you for the time you invested with me. I look forward to following up with you about our next steps.

Dear _____,

Thank you for sharing your ideas and insights with me about XYZ company. I look forward to learning more at our next meeting.

Dear _____,

Thank you for sharing your time with me as we discussed a mutually beneficial business relationship. I look forward to your email outlining our next steps.

The Wide World of Thank-You Notes

Professionally, there are so many opportunities to send a note to extend gratitude and appreciation. Here is my master list of "any occasion" templates to help you get the ball rolling.

New introduction or meeting

Dear _____,

Thank you for scheduling a meeting for us at_____.
I look forward to seeing you [date/time]. If you have
any questions or need additional information, feel
free to contact me.

Dear _____,

Thank you for your kind introduction to _____.
I appreciate you opening the door for me. I will keep
you posted on our progress. If I can be of service
to you or someone you know, feel free to contact
me.

Dear _____,

Thank you for your kind introduction of _____.
I appreciate you and your faith in me.

Dear _____,

Thank you for meeting me at [location/event].
I look forward to following up with you regarding
_____.

Dear _____,

Thank you for spending some time with me at _____. In today's business, time is precious, and you can rest assured I will be respectful of the time you invest with me.

After a business outing (golf, dinner, etc.)

Dear _____,

Thank you for golfing with me at _____. We didn't come close to the course record, but I had fun visiting with you. I look forward to our next round.

Dear _____,

Thank you for your invitation to play _____ course. What a great treat. See you on the green.

Dear _____,

Thank you for your fabulous dinner party at _____. The food was spectacular, and the friends were a delight to visit with. Looking forward to our next time together.

Dear _____,

Thank you for supporting our _____. Friends like you make our group stronger every year.

Enjoyed someone's presentation at a meeting or seminar

Dear _____,

Thank you for sharing your insights at _____. I appreciate you and your commitment to serve others by helping them avoid the mistakes you made. Next time you are in San Diego, let's meet for a beverage.

Dear _____,

Thank you for your great presentation on _____. When can we talk about how we can share your message with more people?

Dear _____,

Thank you for your inspiring message. When can we talk about how we can get you in front of more people?

Congratulations on the new job or promotion

Dear _____,

Congratulations on your success. I appreciate you and the example you set for the rest of us to continually grow and serve others.

Dear _____,

Congratulations on your new job. I know they will love you and your energy. Let's get together and celebrate.

Dear _____,

You got the job! Congratulations—your persistence paid off. When can we get together to celebrate?

Saw a relevant article in the paper/online that someone might appreciate

Dear _____,

I saw this article and I thought of you. Enjoy, and let's catch up soon.

Dear _____,

I saw this article about your industry and thought you would enjoy the information. Let's catch up over coffee soon.

Dear _____,

Your company was in the news. Here is the article for your files. Let's get together soon.

Appreciation to colleague or employee for extra help

Dear _____,

Thank you for stepping up and helping get _____ project done. I appreciate you and your support.

Dear _____,

Thank you for staying late to get my docs out so _____ could sign their docs in the morning instead of tomorrow afternoon. I appreciate you and your customer service.

Dear _____,

Thank you for your feedback on my report. Your suggestions made it better. I appreciate you and your insight. If there is anything I can do to support you, feel free to ask me.

Announcement of someone's family member's success—sending an extra copy

Dear _____,

Congratulations! I saw your daughter in the news and thought you would like a copy for your scrapbook. Let's catch up soon.

Dear _____,

I saw this article in the paper about your son winning the science fair and thought you would want a copy for posterity. See you at the grocery store.

Dear _____,

Congratulations on your dad's promotion to director at the hospital. Stay well and let's catch up soon.

Connecting with customers and suppliers

Dear _____,

Thank you for getting my part to me on time. I appreciate you and your follow-through. If I can

be of service to you or someone you know, feel free
to contact me.

Dear _____,

Thank you for your excellent service. I appreciate
you and your attention to detail in making sure
my order was complete. If I can be of service
to you or someone you know, feel free to contact
me.

Dear _____,

Thank you for giving us the opportunity to serve you.
I look forward to working with you to accomplish
your goal of _____. If you have any questions or
know someone else I can serve, feel free to contact
me.

Dear _____,

Thank you for your inquiry into working with me.
I look forward to working with you to accomplish
your _____ goals. If you have any questions
or need additional information, feel free to contact
me.

Grateful for an opportunity or for some great service provided

Dear _____,

Thank you for your excellent service. It is gratifying to see someone dedicated to doing a good job. Your efforts are sincerely appreciated. If my company or I can serve you in any way, feel free to call me.

Dear _____,

Thank you for your outstanding care of my car and getting me back on the road. I appreciate you and your attention to detail. If I can ever be of service to you or someone you know, feel free to contact me.

Dear _____,

Thank you for your excellent care of my clothes. I know I can count on you to make my clothes look great. If I can ever be of service to you or someone you know, feel free to contact me.

Dear _____,

Thank you for giving me the opportunity to serve your _____ needs. It was a pleasure working with you to accomplish your goals. If you have any questions or know someone else I can serve, feel free to contact me.

Offering support for loss of a job

Dear _____,

Sorry to hear about your layoff. If you need someone to talk to, feel free to reach out to me. Know I am thinking about you and ready to serve you.

Dear _____,

Bummer! I can't believe they let you go. If you need someone to talk to or yell with, feel free to give me a call.

Dear _____,

Ouch! I can't believe they let you go. If you need a recommendation or some ideas to pivot to a new industry, let's get together and talk. Know that you are in my thoughts and prayers.

Recent business opening or celebration of business anniversary

Dear _____,

Congratulations on your new business! You are going to set the world on fire. Let's get together so I can find out how to help you grow your business.

Dear _____,

Happy anniversary! Let's celebrate your continued success and catch up. I'll buy the beverage as an anniversary gift! Talk to you soon.

Dear _____,

You did it! Congratulations on opening the doors to your new business! Let's get together to celebrate. You can tell me who the perfect client is for me to send your way so I can help you keep the doors open. See you soon.

Recent promotion or expansion

Dear _____,

Congratulations on your new office location. You have worked hard for your success, and it is paying off. Let's get together to celebrate.

Dear _____,

They promoted you! Congratulations! You deserve it! Let's get together to celebrate.

Dear _____,

Congratulations on your promotion! Your hard work and follow-through have paid off. Let's get together and celebrate.

Dear _____,

Congratulations on your expansion. Your hard work is paying off, and the market appreciates the great service you provide. Let me know when we can catch up.

Award or prize

Dear _____,

Congratulations on winning top agent in your office. Your hard work has paid off. Let's get together and see how we can make next year better.

Dear _____,

Congratulations on winning closest to the pin at the Boys and Girls Club golf tournament. What a shot. See you on the green. If I can be of service to you or someone you know, feel free to contact me.

Dear _____,

Congratulations on landing your marlin! What a story! Wish I had been there. See you on the deck. If I can be of service to you or someone you know, feel free to contact me.

No reason at all

Dear _____,

Thank you for being my friend. I was thinking about you and wanted to let you know you are in my heart, my thoughts, and my prayers. See you soon.

Dear _____,

I was thinking about you and wanted you to know I appreciate you and our friendship. See you soon.

Dear _____,

Thank you for being you. Just a note to let you know I appreciate you and your love of life. You are in my heart, my thoughts, and my prayers.

You can find additional thank you note templates designed specifically for mortgage loan originators at www.stevenalittlefield.com. Regardless of who you are or what business you're in, as you can see, there is always a reason to send a thank-you note.

An Occasion for Gratitude

I've found that gratitude is often its own occasion. When you celebrate it by sending a handwritten thank-you note, you invite even more things to be grateful about into your life.

With these templates in hand, you're just about ready to venture out into the world with the tool of the thank-you note locked and loaded at your side. But I can't let you go without sharing one last strategy—one that has literally been the key to my success and abundance all these years. The next chapter will show you how to magnetize referrals with the power of thank you.

Gratitude Challenge

List five people you haven't talked to in a while whom you appreciate and would like to get back in touch with. Send each of them a handwritten thank-you note.

1. _____

2. _____

3. _____

4. _____

5. _____

Chapter 6

Magnetize Referrals

Feed Your Referrals

When we ran Signature Funding, my partner, Jenjer, and I set up a system: we and our loan officers gave a twenty-five-dollar gift certificate to everyone who gave our company a referral. We figured we'd use the same psychology that casinos use: give players a small reward each time the cherry pops up in a slot machine in order to keep people in the game. Only instead of credits, our reward system was food and drink.

One of our best referral sources was a client and friend of mine named Charles.

Charles knew everyone. His company manufactured custom fixtures for kitchens and bathrooms. He had more than two hundred employees and walked the floor of his factory daily, making sure every detail was being attended to. On average, Charles sent me three or four referrals a month. And for every referral he sent, I sent him a thank-you note with a gift certificate in return.

One day, I popped by his office to chat, and Charles had ten or fifteen of these gift certificates on his desk. He picked them up and handed them to me. "I don't eat at the Brigantine," he said in a practical voice, "so here—give these to someone else and stop sending them to me."

I looked at the stack of certificates, but I paused before I reached out to take them. "Charles," I said. "Do you still walk the floor of your factory?"

"Of course," he answered, surprised.

"Then let me make a suggestion," I said. "Put those gift certificates in your pocket, and let's go walk your floor together. You keep an eye out for anyone who is doing something right. When you see someone doing exceptional work, give the worker one of the certificates as a reward for good service."

Charles agreed to the experiment, and we headed out to the floor. For fun, we found one of his team members, Jorge, who had done an exceptional job polishing a particular piece of hardware. Charles pulled a certificate out of his back pocket and handed it to Jorge. "Good job," he said. "Have dinner on me."

Jorge's eyes lit up with surprise and gratitude. And Charles looked different, too. In a matter of seconds, he had transformed from a hard factory man into an appreciative owner. He was a hero.

Charles kept handing out the certificates, and in no time he noticed that the morale on the floor had risen. He was getting more production and better quality out of his people than he ever had before.

The real kicker is that I myself began to get calls from his people, wanting to find out if they could qualify for a home loan so that I would "have" to send more thank-you notes and more gift certificates to Charles. I probably did thirty home loans for Charles's employees alone.

That's the Law of Reciprocity for you. What you send out into the world comes back to you magnified and multiplied. And nowhere is this truer than with referrals.

Referrals: The Lifeblood of Your Business

Referrals are the lifeblood of your business.

Without a pipeline of referrals, you have to pour huge amounts of energy into finding new leads all the time. Worse, once you find them, you are cold-selling all day, every day. That approach gets tiring fast, and it usually leads to burnout—and the death of your business.

But when you have a steady stream of referrals coming in, all that energy you used to spend getting leads can go into serving instead. Even better, the people you talk to are already coming to you with an open heart and an open mind. Because they were referred by someone they trust, they're willing to have a real conversation with you. Instead of selling them on working with you in the first place, you can spend your time building deeper relationships, and your business will thrive.

Thank-you notes are the most powerful referral-generation tool I have ever known.

Think about it: When do you hear about the service someone received? When it's really great, or really bad. Thank-you notes are a shining symbol of top-notch service. Gratitude, especially in our day and age, is noteworthy. It gets people talking about you and your service. Word-of-mouth advertising is the best advertising you can get. When you impress an individual, he or she can't wait to share news of you. That's just human nature.

The thank-you note is part of the way we serve others, both personally and professionally. It's our way of going the extra mile. Giving excellent service not only strengthens our connections; it also encourages new ones. And when you tap into these bottomless pools of referrals, your success grows exponentially.

Not everyone you send a thank-you note to will be in the position to do business with you. Many of them, however, will know people who are. You can bank on that. And the people you develop the closest relationships with will work overtime building your business for you by sending you referrals.

Remember, referrals aren't just about connecting with other people in your industry. They're about the people of the world who inspire you—the friendly server at your favorite restaurant, or the mechanic who services your car. Do not overlook people simply because they appear to be unlikely clients at the moment. Your dog groomer may be your secret weapon sometime down the line. You just can't know.

In this chapter, I'll share my favorite thank-you note referral templates with you and show you how sending notes even when you don't think anything will come of it can result in amazing things.

The Referral Templates

The most important time to send a thank-you note is immediately after receiving a referral.

When I say "immediately after," I mean it. There's a reason you send a thank-you note before calling the referent. Writing a handwritten thank-you note sets you up to be grateful for the referral. When you are grateful, you're far less likely to focus on the outcome—on what will eventually transpire with the referent.

At Signature Funding, we found that if loan officers waited until after they talked to the referent to send the thank-you note and gift certificate to the referring Realtor, they weren't nearly as motivated to do it—particularly if the referent only had a loan question and didn't actually need a new loan.

Sending thank-you notes to the people who refer business

to you reinforces good behavior. Forget to appreciate your referral sources, and you kill the golden goose.

Here are a few of my favorite thank-you note templates to use for referrals:

Dear _____,

Thank you for your kind referral of _____. You can rest assured that anyone you refer to me will receive the highest degree of professional service possible. If you have any questions or know someone else I can serve, feel free to contact me.

Dear _____,

Thank you for your kind referral of _____. I appreciate you and your trust in me. I will keep you updated on our progress. If you have any questions or know someone else I can serve, feel free to contact me.

Dear _____,

Thank you for your kind referral of _____. I appreciate you and your faith in me. I look forward to taking great care of _____'s financing needs. I will keep you posted on our progress.

Dear _____,

Thank you for your kind referral of _____. I am grateful for you and your trust in me to provide _____ the best service possible. I will keep you posted on our progress.

More Than the Money

Even if your thank-you notes don't always directly pay off in more business, they can reward you in other ways.

I once played in a five-day golf tournament in which foursomes of golfers got to play with a different celebrity each day of the event. On the first day, my buddy Don and I were paired with Mike Reno, the lead singer of Loverboy, and Tunes, the saxophonist for the Beaver Brown Band. We had such a great day of golf—laughing and telling stories together—that Mike ended up asking the tournament director if he could play with us the rest of the week. The tournament gave him permission as long as he asked us. After some good-natured ribbing, we told him of course he could, and for the next three days we had a blast together.

After the tournament, we all exchanged our contact information and went our separate ways.

And this is precisely the place where the train can come right off the tracks. This is the place where the business card usually gets tossed, the phone information buried, the opportunity ignored.

When I got home, however, I sent a handwritten thank-you note to everyone I had met, including Mike Reno. And a few days later, I got a text from Mike.

"Thank you for your note," it said. "I have toured the world and met some great people, and you are the only person I have ever received a handwritten thank you note from. I'm going to be playing in Beaumont and we're coming in a day early. Can you come up and play golf and then go to the show with us?"

Of course I joined them, played a great game of golf, and met the rest of his bandmates. When they played in Atlanta, I flew out and stayed with my buddy Don and his family. We took Mike golfing before the concert and then Don and I took his wife, Valerie, and five of her high school girlfriends to the concert, with backstage passes and camera access. I was a hero.

Ten years later, I'm still getting texts from Mike telling me when he's going to be playing in LA or any other city in California. He always says he's looking forward to seeing me, and vice versa. I get to be friends with a literal rock star. All because of one handwritten thank-you note.

Send Notes Anyway

Life is not just about getting the job or the piece of business. There are times when it makes sense to send personal thank-you notes with nothing in mind other than showing someone appreciation. These personal notes often lead to amazing relationships that can benefit you (and them) in untold ways.

I'm always on the lookout for people I can send a thank-you note to outside of the business arena. Here are a few examples of opportunities I've spotted:

- I was referred to an auto glass installation company, where I took my friend's truck to have the molding replaced. I sent a thank-you note to the owner of that company, the installer, and the friend who had referred me. The owner of the window company referred an associate to me—a man who fixed auto air conditioners—for a refinance loan.

- I met a server who was studying mechanical engineering at San Diego State University who was just fabulous. I sent her a thank-you note. The next time I stopped by, she gushed with appreciation and introduced me to her manager, who proceeded to buy me a beer. So I sent the manager a thank-you note, and another one to the server as well. How do you think they will treat me next time I stop in?

- I checked into a hotel, and the reservation specialist waived my parking fee to apologize for the fact that my room wasn't ready. I sent her a thank-you note. She sent me an email expressing her gratitude for my thoughtfulness and demanded that the next time I stay at her property to let her know.

- I was introduced to the manager at the Omni Club in Petco Park. I sent her a thank-you note, and she sent me an email telling me that any time I'm at Petco Park I should pop in and have a beer.

- I was at a charity function where I was introduced to a guy who worked for Coca-Cola. I sent him a thank-you note, and he emailed me back a thank-you. We carried on a correspondence and reconnected at different charity events around San Diego. He is now the EVP for Bacardi, and he invites me to more events than I can possibly fit into my schedule.

The stories are literally endless, so I will distill it down to the lowest common denominator for you: If someone makes you smile or laugh, or causes you to feel good, appreciated, heard, comforted, joyful, respected, or just plain comfortable, *send that person a handwritten thank-you note.* You won't regret it. Trust me.

The Boat Mechanic

Ed, my boat mechanic, was opening a thank-you note from me when a client of his came in. Ed finished reading the card and then put it down on the counter so he could talk to the client.

They talked about the services the client needed for his boat. Then the client nodded at my card on the counter. "You know," he said, "I'm looking to refinance my house. Do you think this guy would be a good person to talk to?"

Ed stepped right up and told him that I had done Ed's own home loan, several of his mechanics' home loans, several of his customers' home loans, and yes, I would definitely be a good guy for him to talk to. Ed handed him my card.

Just like that, I was able to fund another loan—and send out another thank-you card with another gift certificate, this time to my boat mechanic, Ed.

Regardless of how big Signature Funding became, I always sent a thank-you note to the service manager, the receptionist, my boat mechanics—everyone I met. And almost every time, I'd get a referral or two from them to serve a mutual client.

It worked like magic.

Treat your referrals right, and they will bring you all the business you could ever want. That's the lesson here. And it all begins with the handwritten thank-you note.

Thank-you notes are great beginnings that inspire endless

possibilities. In the last chapter, I'll give you a taste of the places gratitude can really take you—and beyond.

Gratitude Challenge

List five people who have recently referred business to you. Send each of them a handwritten thank-you note.

1. _____

2. _____

3. _____

4. _____

5. _____

Chapter 7

Gratitude Attracts Abundance

Nuclear-Proof

Business was booming.

Each day, I stopped in to a bunch of local real estate offices and chatted with my friends there—the agents—about the Super Bowl, football trades, and the NBA. Only on my way out would I put rate sheets in their cubby-hole mailboxes. All of these agents were people I had first sent thank-you notes to, who had sent business my way.

I would soon learn how valuable these relationships really were.

One Saturday in April of 1986, after a stretch of incredible success with my business, the world woke up to the Chernobyl nuclear disaster.

It was as if life as we knew it had come to an end. That Monday, the stock market didn't open. Banks weren't wiring funds. The economic machine ground to a stop. We were all in a daze. By the end of that week, rates had jumped from 8.5 to 10 percent. All of my "locks" had expired, and the loans I had arranged were cancelled.

My pipeline was devastated.

I'd been so excited about my pipeline. I had been doing so well that I'd bought a BMW 325i convertible for my twenty-fourth birthday just the month before. Now, I wouldn't be able to afford the thing anymore. *No one will want to borrow money at 10 percent when the rate was at 8.5 percent just a few days ago,* I thought.

That day, my boss, Clay, told me that if I would deliver my flyers to my real estate offices as usual, he would give me one hundred dollars for every flyer I could find from any other lender, as long as I met him at Spoons by 5:00 p.m. When I showed up, my hands were empty. He offered to buy me dinner and cocktails for my effort. I drank like it was my last night on earth. Everything I'd worked for—by getting to work early, going the extra mile, and studying anything I could get my hands on—was down the drain. None of my hard work had made a damn bit of difference. I was going to have to get a different career. I felt like all was lost—again!

I don't remember getting home, wasted as I was. When I came to, it was 9:30 in the morning—and someone was pounding on my front door.

Still dressed in the same clothes from the day before, I stumbled out of bed and opened the door. Standing there on my doorstep was Carol, our receptionist. "What do you want?" I asked, like a truculent child.

"Clay sent me to fetch you," Carol said, giving me a look. "You need to get your butt into the office ASAP."

Hung over, I managed to shower, put on a suit and tie, and stagger into the office an hour later. When I got there, Carol was waiting for me again. She handed me a stack of message slips at the door. "The phone has been ringing off the hook for you all morning," she said.

I looked around. None of the other loan officers had shown up to work. They were all hiding.

Nauseated, my head still pounding, I started returning the calls. Every agent I talked to said the same thing to me: "Thank God someone is working."

I talked to agents all day long, set appointments, called their referrals to do prequalifications, and set appointments to take loan applications. Sometime in the late afternoon, it finally hit me.

I'd had it all wrong. People care about whom they're working with and who can help them accomplish their goals first, and the cost to accomplish their goals second.

This was the day I got wise. I wasn't in the interest rate business. I was in the people business.

No matter how bleak it is, if you put gratitude and effort out into the world, you're going to get results. You're going to be nuclear-proof. And when that happens, the possibilities of where you can go with your life are truly endless.

Grow, Grow, Grow

In my business, if you follow the system I've just taught you to build relationships with real estate agents, then you will have a consistent referral source of borrowers. If you have a consistent source of borrowers to work with, you have a consistent source of loans. If you have a consistent pipeline of loans, you can build a business. And if you build a business that puts people first, you will have a sustainable business that can grow and grow and grow.

But remember that your business isn't the only thing that grows when you put gratitude to work for you, in your life. You grow, too.

An old adage asks, "Have you been in the business thirty years, or one year thirty times?" The person who is constantly growing and learning is the person who will succeed not just in business, but in building a joyful life.

The bigger you build your house of gratitude, the more room you have to fill it with abundance.

If you aren't growing as a person, you're dying. Always choose growth. And remember that gratitude is the Miracle-Gro for a happy, thriving existence.

The Question of "Enough"

Happiness can be elusive for us humans.

Hundreds of books come out each year that address how

to be happy. "Happy," for me, is all about gratitude. The opposite of gratitude is scarcity—feeling like you never have enough.

A feeling of scarcity turns us into consumers. Consumption is the very underpinning of our society. When we're consuming, we find that it's never enough, whatever "it" represents.

We eat a pound of peanut M&Ms, instead of just one, thinking that we'll get more of the experience that way, and yet we don't. McMansions, 7-Eleven's sixty-four-ounce Double Gulp, bigger yachts, the Hummer, the latest iPhone, more wine, more food, more sex—it's all the same. We've fallen into the mindset that more is better, more will satisfy us, and we hope that more is more, but it isn't. It never is. Underneath it all, we're afraid that we're not going to get it all in, that someone will take it from us.

Yet, if you look around, you can see that you have enough already. That you need no more.

What do you really *need* right now? Are you in touch with that? What would it be like to acknowledge that you're getting what you need—that you're complete? What would support your sense of wholeness?

Coming from that place of completeness, what more do you want?

Each day, I wake up and I ask myself three questions: What can I do to be happy today? What can I learn today? And what can I teach today?

Every time I answer them, I know that the answers are things that I already have access to. I have and I am enough. That alone is something to be grateful for.

A Mindful Note

I've taught you almost everything I know about the handwritten thank-you note. But there is one more piece of advice I'd like to leave you with. Something that goes a little deeper, past the simple act of writing.

When you write your notes, strive to be both present and grateful.

In today's business world, we keep piling on things to do. Then, in order to get everything done, we end up cutting corners. We tend to use time-saving devices so we can do more, instead of using them to spend more time with the people around us. How many times have you been in a car with the opportunity to spend one-on-one time with a friend, a significant other, or your children and, instead of talking to the person beside you, you talk on the phone to someone else?

Give yourself permission to take a step back. Open your mind up to being present where you are, whether you are connecting with others in person on a meaningful level or connecting with them in words through your thank-you notes. Remember, every time you send a note,

- you are imprinting on your subconscious mind that you are thankful.

- you get to share that thankfulness with another human being, which feels good for everybody involved.

- the person who receives your note feels appreciated by your thoughtfulness.

- you increase your awareness to look for people to meet, know, and be thankful for.

- you attract more like-minded people to you—people who are equally thankful.

- you're able to grow your business.

- you are able to build deeper, more meaningful relationships.

When you are present with your note writing, you turn a simple act of gratitude into something extraordinary.

Never forget that the Law of Attraction works on the principle of "what you ask for, you will receive." The concept of "asking" is not just about thinking and hoping that something will come true. It requires positive, purposeful, mindful action.

This is what a thank-you note truly is: gratitude in action.

The more grateful you are in feeling and in action, the more you will have to be grateful for, and the more abundance will fill your life.

The Taste of Success

You can achieve all the material wealth you want in life. But without people you love to share it with, none of it has meaning.

When I got married, my wife, Jenjer, and I chose to buy a house in La Jolla. It had a big kitchen off the garage, and a casual dining area with French doors that opened onto a patio overlooking the pool and a Jacuzzi built for twenty-five—along with a formal dining room that seated twelve. The wide courtyard had a waterfall at the far end surrounded by lush tropical palms and birds of paradise. The formal living room led to the family room, which, combined, seated an additional eight people. There were three big guest rooms with their own bathrooms, a master suite, a gym, and a meditation room that opened up to a balcony overlooking the waterfall. We had fireplaces, wrap couches, and windows showcasing the Pacific Ocean only a block away.

Now, that's a lot of house for two people and two dogs. It might even sound extravagant. But do you know why we chose it?

We chose it because it was a beautiful place to entertain all of the people we loved.

In particular, I wanted a home where we could comfortably host Thanksgiving. Growing up, Thanksgiving was my favorite holiday. Everyone in my family loved it.

Each year, Mom made not just the turkey, but all of the fixings: mashed potatoes, butternut squash, yams, Hawaiian King rolls, cranberry sauce, black olives (which fit very well on my fingertips), green beans with French onions on top, peas, and whole steamed carrots. My uncle, a Seventh-day Adventist minister, would always gasp as my mom brought in the turkey. "Look at the size of that breast— I mean bird!" he would say, and we'd all fall on the floor laughing.

Silly, I know, but what can I say?

I loved Thanksgiving—because of the people who gathered for it.

So when we bought our house, we knew it had to be large enough to accommodate the entire Thanksgiving crew: my mom and dad, my sister and her husband and daughter, my brother Fred and his wife and four children, and my other brother David and his partner. My uncle and aunt also came along, as did my cousins and our good friends, such as the Vargas and Hollingshead families I had grown up with. One year, we invited my birth mother, Judy, and her daughter, Tracy. There were dogs and kids and new pals who had been invited by somebody or another.

Everyone was welcome. We meant it when we said the more people, the merrier. We had all the space we needed. The more love, the merrier.

To me, that's what success really tastes like.

A Note a Day

If you write just one thank-you note a day, you will have 365 deeper relationships by the end of the year.

Now consider that if you write just five notes a day, that number jumps to more than 1,800 deeper relationships. Can you imagine how grateful you would feel with 1,800 more meaningful relationships in your life?

Are you ready to get started?

When you're ready to embark on your gratitude journey, you don't have to do it alone. I have built a community of entrepreneurs who share our belief in the power of "thank you," and we would love for you to join us. You can get involved with our online program or join us in person at one of my half-day workshops. I also give talks on the business of thank you around the world. To learn more, visit www. stevenalittlefield.com.

You can also take our free week-long Gratitude Challenge. Write thank-you notes for a week, track your results, and share your results with our community at www.stevenalittlefield. com. I bet you'll get more than you bargained for.

That's just how gratitude works.

Choose One Thing

Pick one thing to be grateful about. Now, say it: "Thank you."

Then do it again. Choose one person you're grateful for. Thank that person by sending him or her a handwritten thank-you note. Say it: "I'm grateful that you're part of my life." Just write one thank-you note; let one person you've met know that you appreciate him or her. Put that one little ripple out there in the cosmic pond.

How does it feel? Pretty good, right?

Are you ready to do it again?

Gratitude is a choice. Not a casual choice, but one that will allow you to design a life of love and connection. A life that gives you a sense of purpose, not just an existence where you show up each day for a twelve-hour shift in some cubicle, surrounded by people you'd rather avoid if you could, chasing the almighty dollar.

Gratitude is the bedrock on which you build your personal version of success. Brick by brick. One thank-you note at a time.

This is your call to action. It's time for you to grow your own business—your own life. You've got the system. You understand the philosophy behind it all. Start small, if you have to. Commit to just one handwritten thank-you note per day. Ask yourself whom you can be grateful for today. Share your stories at www.stevenalittlefield.com.

Everything starts with gratitude—with a sense and show of appreciation. It's really that simple.

So what are you waiting for?

Put your pen to paper right now. Send one handwritten thank-you note. Track the response you get from it.

And watch the gratitude that comes back to you multiplied in ways you can't even imagine.

ABOUT THE AUTHOR

Steven Littlefield is a leader in the mortgage loan industry and the founder of Infinite Fundings. If Steven isn't teaching, traveling, or typing out his thoughts for his next book, you can usually find him golfing at Torrey Pines, or scuba diving off the Lois Ann. To learn more about his *Business of Gratitude* training programs or to keep in touch, visit www.stevenalittlefield.com or send an email to steven@stevenalittlefield.com. Littlefield lives in Del Mar, California, where he spends his mornings walking on the beach and his evenings either enjoying a glass of wine at Sbicca or watching a game at Jimmy O's, always asking the all-important question: What are you grateful for today?